Getting to Know Me

Encouraging Positive Attitudes in Children

John Taylor

 David Fulton Publishers

David Fulton Publishers Ltd
The Chiswick Centre, 414 Chiswick High Road, London W4 5TF

www.fultonpublishers.co.uk

David Fulton Publishers is a division of Granada Learning Limited, part of ITV plc.

British Library Cataloguing in Publication Data
A catalogue record for this book is available from the British Library.

ISBN: 1 84312 414 9

10 9 8 7 6 5 4 3 2 1

Typeset by FiSH Books, Enfield
Printed and bound in Great Britain

Contents

BULLYING ISSUES

Introduction

The field of education, particularly in recent years, has many prescriptive tomes on what should be taught, when and how. Professional experience and skills clearly mark respected academics and educationalists as experts in their specialised subjects. However, education is about those on the receiving end; otherwise it is pointless. You, the teacher, are the *significant* expert. You *know* your students – their needs, foibles and interests. You know the best way of engaging and motivating them. You plan around your knowledge of their prior learning and attitudes, both positive and negative, adapting to their needs. Some students carry emotional baggage that you may be aware of, which needs to be accommodated in your approach.

This book is not a teaching scheme. It is a source of materials which you can either slot into your own programmes of study for class or group teaching, or use one to one as part of an individualised behaviour modification programme.

For a number of years I worked with a behaviour support team, helping to change or adapt the attitudes of both pupils at risk of permanent exclusion and, occasionally, those of a handful of unenlightened teachers. Finding appropriate copiable resources was time consuming, trawling through a number of published schemes to pick out the good from the mediocre, the current from the dated. This is the book I wish I'd had.

Getting to Know Me includes a sample one-to-one anger management programme plus a blank form for assembling programmes of your own, tailored to the needs of groups or individuals.

The notes which accompany the activities are only intended as a guide to be adapted to your needs. For instance, when used one to one with a pupil, the adult may have to be more open and share his or her own experiences during discussion without being dogmatic about his/her own views.

UNIT 1: INTRODUCING ME (1)

MAIN FOCUS: CREATING A PERSONAL SNAPSHOT BY DISCUSSING AND LISTING A FEW PREFERENCES

First box

Discuss names: given, abbreviated, altered (e.g. 'Kazza' or 'Kaz' instead of 'Karen'). Other nicknames including derogatory ones, 'pet' names, etc. What do your prefer friends to call you?

Remaining boxes

If working one to one, discuss own preferences and compare to theirs.

If working with a group or class, allow a few minutes discussion with one or two others before each is completed.

Watching

Who watches TV because it's there and switched on most of the time?

Who only watches specific programmes?

Listening

Discuss styles of music, encourage discussion about the target audience for different types of music.

Sport

Make the distinction between active participation and passive watching.

Who attends the event and who just views on television?

Are they active or armchair fans?

How many Manchester United fans have ever been to Old Trafford?

Other interests

Discuss types of hobbies and interests: active (e.g. skateboarding, fishing); passive (e.g. collecting things, computer games); creative (e.g. making things).

PLENARY

Highlight differences and everyone's right to be accepted as a 'me'.

UNIT 1: INTRODUCING ME (1)

My name is .... D.O.B. ....

I like my friends to call me ....

My favourite place is ....

I like eating ....

Watching

I enjoy watching   television ❑   videos/DVDs ❑   films ❑

My favourite is ....

I enjoy reading   books ❑   magazines ❑

comics ❑   newspapers ❑

My favourite is ....

Listening

I enjoy listening to   solo singers ❑   groups ❑

My favourite singer or group is ....

My favourite style of music is ....

Sport

I like to watch ....

I like to play ....

Other interests

In my spare time I like to ....

UNIT 2: INTRODUCING ME (2)

MAIN FOCUS: CREATING A PERSONAL SNAPSHOT BY DISCUSSING AND LISTING A FEW PREFERENCES

Allow discussion in twos or threes before completing the boxes. Tackle one box at a time, briefing before and drawing together some responses afterwards.

Top box

Discuss how names used by friends are sometimes different from your 'real' name. Names used indicate the relationship a person has with you.

Middle box

This box is intended to include an issue, habit or characteristic that really annoys. Give a few examples that vary in seriousness (e.g. people who chew gum with mouth open, pollution, discrimination, global warming, etc.).

Bottom box

Brainstorm personal characteristics, both positive and negative.

Brainstorm living people whom individuals admire (they don't have to be famous).

Brainstorm people from history whom individuals admire.

Point out the 'because...' sections.

PLENARY

Discuss which personal characteristics are admired most or least. Point out that we all have a set of varied characteristics which can annoy or please.

UNIT 2: INTRODUCING ME (2)

My name is ....

My friends call me...

If I could change my appearance I'd prefer...

My idea of a perfect holiday would be..

....

My idea of a perfect meal would be..

....

My greatest fear is...

.... makes me angry because...............................

....

....

I like people who...

I don't like people who ....

I admire people who..

....

The living person I admire most is ....because

....

A person I admire from history is...because

....

UNIT 3: HOW DO I FEEL ABOUT...?

MAIN FOCUS: EXPRESSING PERSONAL OPINIONS ABOUT A RANGE OF ISSUES

Explain that the face symbols should be drawn at the top of each box, small enough to leave space for a reaction or comment.

Discuss one row at a time, briefing to make sure everyone understands what the box titles mean.

Allow twos or threes to discuss each issue briefly.

Before briefing for the next row, get feedback and reactions, encouraging acknowledgement of, and respect for, contrary views. Play 'devil's advocate' by proposing counter-arguments.

The last two rows include boxes for pupils to insert personal preferences.

PLENARY

Draw together the varied range of opinions on each issue, particularly those which are 'grey'. Where there appears to be consensus, play 'devil's advocate', e.g. factory farming produces affordable food.

UNIT 3: HOW DO I FEEL ABOUT...?

How do you feel about...?

Mark the boxes   ☺ = happy   ☹ = angry   ☺ = no interest or worry

Give reasons

Pollution	Waste	Litter	Recycling

Cruelty to children	Cruelty to animals	Factory farming	World poverty

Watching .... (a sport)	Taking part in .... (a sport)	Listening to music	Performing music

Watching .... (a TV soap)	.... (a hobby)	Computer games	Surfing the internet

UNIT 4: HOW DO I *FEEL* WHEN...?

MAIN FOCUS: EXPRESSING PERSONAL FEELINGS TO SITUATIONS

Discuss a variety of feelings such as fear, embarrassment, shyness, anger, happiness, pride, feeling important, feeling valued, feeling put down or ignored etc.

Point out that answers require more detail than a single-word response.

Take each 'When...' statement and invite students to suggest how they would feel. If appropriate, share your own feelings and compare them to the pupils' feelings.

Tackle the 'Well done!' sentences together, ascertaining whether who says it makes the feeling different.

Discuss who a stranger might be (shop manager when making a complaint, an official, Ofsted inspector, school governor).

Highlight differing reactions to the two 'told off' sentences.

PLENARY

Draw together the range of feelings experienced in different situations and how some of these can be physical, e.g. stomach discomfort, part of our caveman 'fight or flight' reflex.

UNIT 4: HOW DO I *FEEL* WHEN...?

When someone insults me I feel...

When someone calls me something nice I feel...
....

When a teacher says 'Well done!' I feel...
....

When a friend says 'Well done!' I feel..
....

When I have to approach and speak to a stranger I feel ....
....

When I see someone mistreat an animal I feel ....
....

When I see someone being picked on I feel..
....

When I don't agree with an adult's decision I feel...
....

When I'm told off for something I did do I feel..
....

When I'm told off for something I didn't do I feel..
....

When I know I'm going to be late I feel...
....

When someone interrupts me when I'm talking I feel ....
....

UNIT 5: WHAT DO I *DO* WHEN...?

MAIN FOCUS: EXPRESSING PERSONAL REACTIONS TO SITUATIONS

Discuss the difference between how you react to a situation and how you *feel* about it.

Discuss the difference between spontaneous reactions which may be regretted, and controlled reactions which may mask your true feelings.

Point out that answers require more detail than a single word response.

Discuss each 'When...' statement.

Take each 'When...' statement and invite suggestions of 'gut' and considered responses.

Share how you might react on impulse and how you might react if you have time to think about consequences.

For the two 'told off' sentences discuss the importance of using a careful, considered response to avoid making the situation worse.

PLENARY

Draw attention to how hard it can be to hold back and think before responding to a situation.

Which responses make you feel better?

Which show that we've evolved a little from our caveman ancestors?

UNIT 5: WHAT DO I *DO* WHEN...?

When someone insults me I..

When someone calls me something nice I..
....

When a teacher says 'Well done!' I...
....

When a friend says 'Well done!' I..
....

When I have to approach and speak to a stranger I..
....

When I see someone mistreat an animal I...
....

When I see someone being picked on I...
....

When I don't agree with an adult's decision I...
....

When I'm told off for something I did do I..
....

When I'm told off for something I didn't do I...
....

When I know I'm going to be late I...
....

When someone interrupts me when I'm talking I...
....

UNIT 6: WHO KNOWS WHAT ABOUT ME? (1)

MAIN FOCUS: CONSIDERING DIFFERENT DOMAINS OF INFORMATION

Discuss that different groups know different things about us. Neighbours may only know your name and what they can see.

Family think they know all about you, but perhaps they don't know secrets that you share with friends.

Brainstorm some of the types of things that groups will know about you (name, address, likes, dislikes, activities, personality, etc.).

Point out that some things will be known by more than one group, and so care is needed to write in the correct part of the Venn diagram.

Share a few harmless facts about yourself which are known/not known to different groups. Mark them on an A3 version of the sheet.

Pupils can record facts (e.g. 'I am a judo black belt', 'My Dad is a window cleaner') or else indicate the nature of information (e.g. 'What my bedroom looks like', 'What I watch on TV').

If working with a group or class, stop after a few minutes and invite pupils to share what they have written in the sections, why they have put them there and why the other group(s) would not know that fact.

PLENARY

Different groups know different information about us: a neighbour may not know your name but may recognise you as one of a group of street skateboarders; your friend may know some of the things you get up to which you wouldn't tell your family; your family know things you wouldn't like your friends to know (e.g. you still sleep with your teddy?).

UNIT 6: WHO KNOWS WHAT ABOUT ME? (1)

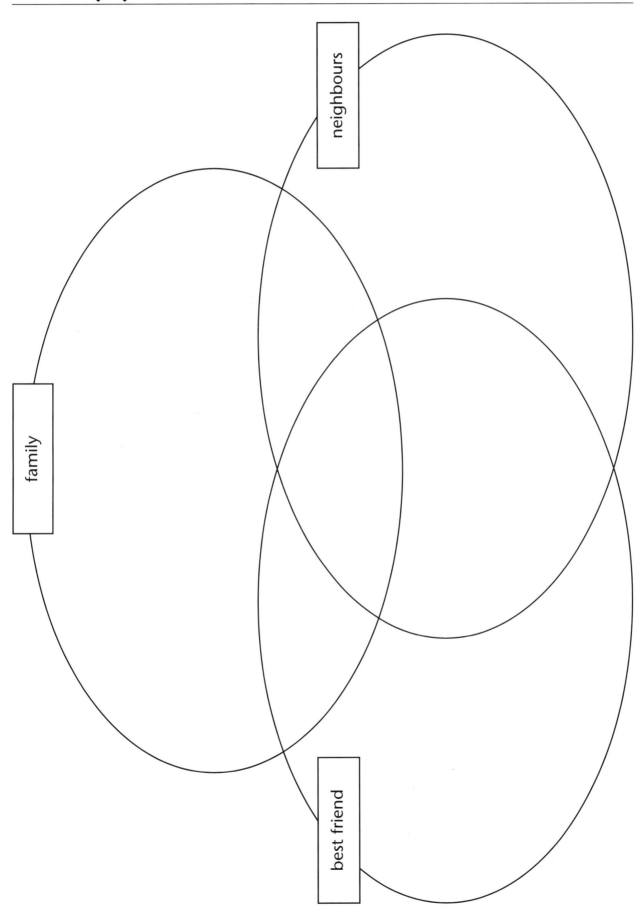

neighbours

family

best friend

UNIT 7: WHO KNOWS WHAT ABOUT ME? (2)

MAIN FOCUS: KNOWLEDGE WHICH MAY BE GENERALLY KNOWN, RESTRICTED OR NOT KNOWN AT ALL

Look carefully at the Carroll diagram and the column and row headings.

Discuss the notion of information that is known to some but not others. For example, school may have information about tests you haven't yet done. No-one really knows your future.

Look at each cell of the diagram. Brainstorm types of information which could go into them.

Top left

This is the only box which can include specific facts such as name, age, address, appearance, exam options, hobbies, likes, dislikes etc.

Top right

People's true opinions of you; information kept secret from you (e.g. special birthday present, exam questions, confidential reports).

Bottom left

This is the 'hidden Me' – my own world, thoughts and feelings kept from everyone else. No facts can be written in this box because they would then be known to others. Instead, it can only contain types of knowledge such as my private thoughts, secrets, day-dreams, guilty secrets).

Bottom right

No-one knows any facts to go in this box, though fortune-tellers will try to convince you that they know. These are the big questions: What will I achieve in life? Will I have children, success, health, long life etc.?

PLENARY

Your true self is made up of knowns and unknowns. Others cannot see your true, inner, secret self; it's a place where your imagination can run wild and your mind can hide from others. It is the secret self which determines why you do things.

UNIT 7: WHO KNOWS WHAT ABOUT ME? (2)

	Things known by me	Things not known by me
Things known by others	*Things known by myself and others*	*Things known by others but not by me*
Things not known by others	*Things known by me but not by others*	*Things no-one knows about me*

UNIT 8: HOW DO I SEE ME? (1)

MAIN FOCUS: PERCEPTIONS OF HOW OTHERS SEE YOU

Point out that people have different opinions about someone's personality.

Personality is a complicated mixture of characteristics, here are just eight character traits represented by scale lines. The zero point in the centre represents 'normal', not extreme in any particular way.

Look at the first scale line pointing out that the zero point is 'normal', and then compare two extremes, 'calm' (−5) and 'very lively' (+5).

Look at the two extremes. Describe the sort of a person who is 'calm' and compare to someone who is 'very lively'.

Mark a tick to show where you think you should be on the scale.

Look at the remaining scales and give examples of the extremes.

Mark the remaining scale lines.

Are you happy with where you have placed yourself? If not, place a question mark on the scales to represent how you would like to be.

Is there anything positive you can do to get there?

PLENARY

Look at the scale markings of a few volunteers. Do people agree with how they have rated themselves? Give reasons why/why not.

Other people only see certain aspects of a person's life and base their opinion on what they see. They cannot see the whole 'you'.

UNIT 8: HOW DO I SEE ME? (1)

Put a ✓ where you think you are now.

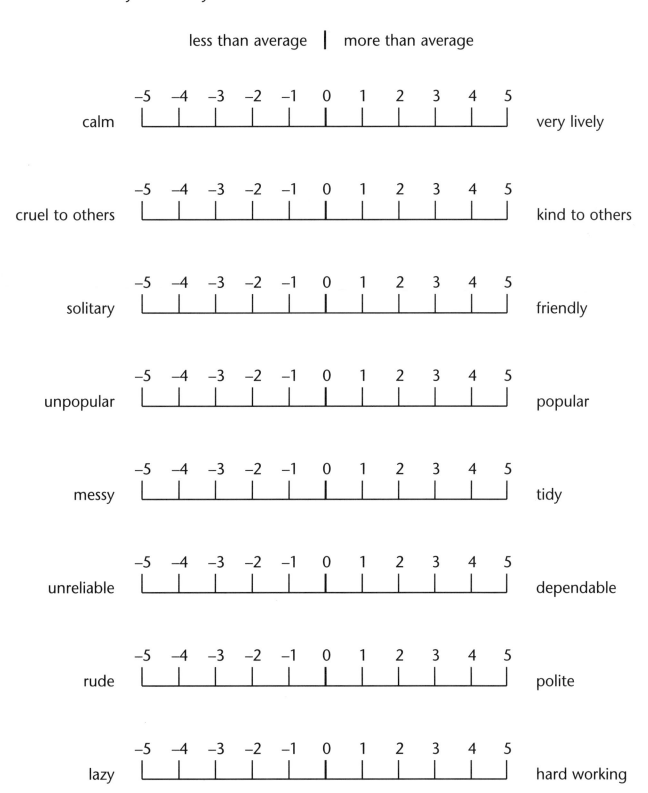

less than average | more than average

| calm | −5 −4 −3 −2 −1 0 1 2 3 4 5 | very lively |

| cruel to others | −5 −4 −3 −2 −1 0 1 2 3 4 5 | kind to others |

| solitary | −5 −4 −3 −2 −1 0 1 2 3 4 5 | friendly |

| unpopular | −5 −4 −3 −2 −1 0 1 2 3 4 5 | popular |

| messy | −5 −4 −3 −2 −1 0 1 2 3 4 5 | tidy |

| unreliable | −5 −4 −3 −2 −1 0 1 2 3 4 5 | dependable |

| rude | −5 −4 −3 −2 −1 0 1 2 3 4 5 | polite |

| lazy | −5 −4 −3 −2 −1 0 1 2 3 4 5 | hard working |

Now put a ? where you'd like to be.

UNIT 9: HOW DO I SEE ME? (2)

MAIN FOCUS: LOOKING AT ONE'S OWN SELF-PERCEPTIONS AND THE IMAGE ONE WOULD LIKE TO PROJECT

Discuss what each of the eight characteristics means, particularly making the distinction between physical and moral courage. Give examples of each. Interpret 'generosity' as being generosity of spirit rather than of pocket.

What sort of person would score a 5 for 'physical courage', 'moral courage', etc.? Can anyone name real people who would score a 5?

Point out that often people try to give an impression that is different from reality.

Take one characteristic at a time, ask them to think and then mark the set of ratings for physical courage.

Invite pupils to ask the person next to them if they agree with the 'How I think others see me' rating.

Complete the remaining seven characteristics, one at a time if preferred.

PLENARY

Share the ratings of a few who volunteer to share them. Do other people agree with their self-rating? Would anyone score them higher?

Who would like others to have a better opinion of them? If others think you are better than you think you are, who is right?

UNIT 9: HOW DO I SEE ME? (2)

Rate your characteristics on a scale of 0 to 5.

0   1   2   3   4   5

How I see myself: ☐☐☐☐☐
How I **think** others see me: ☐☐☐☐☐ **physical**
How I'd **like** others to see me: ☐☐☐☐☐ **courage**

How I see myself: ☐☐☐☐☐
How I **think** others see me: ☐☐☐☐☐ **moral**
How I'd **like** others to see me: ☐☐☐☐☐ **courage**

How I see myself: ☐☐☐☐☐
How I **think** others see me: ☐☐☐☐☐ **patience**
How I'd **like** others to see me: ☐☐☐☐☐

How I see myself: ☐☐☐☐☐
How I **think** others see me: ☐☐☐☐☐ **tolerance**
How I'd **like** others to see me: ☐☐☐☐☐

How I see myself: ☐☐☐☐☐
How I **think** others see me: ☐☐☐☐☐ **empathy**
How I'd **like** others to see me: ☐☐☐☐☐

How I see myself: ☐☐☐☐☐
How I **think** others see me: ☐☐☐☐☐ **ambition**
How I'd **like** others to see me: ☐☐☐☐☐

How I see myself: ☐☐☐☐☐
How I **think** others see me: ☐☐☐☐☐ **honesty**
How I'd **like** others to see me: ☐☐☐☐☐

How I see myself: ☐☐☐☐☐
How I **think** others see me: ☐☐☐☐☐ **generosity**
How I'd **like** others to see me: ☐☐☐☐☐

UNIT 10: HOW DO OTHERS SEE ME?

MAIN FOCUS: PERCEPTIONS OF HOW OTHERS SEE YOU

Point out that each individual is the only person who sees themself in every aspect of life. Everyone else has to base their opinion of you on the part of your life they see.

If you used sheet 8, explain that this time they have to predict how other people would rate them. Otherwise, look at the first scale line, pointing out that the zero point is 'normal', and then compare two extremes, 'calm' (−5) and 'very lively' (+5).

Where on the scale would you place yourself?

Now mark a letter F where your best friend would place you.

Look quickly at the other scale lines, describing what someone at each extreme might be like. Mark the other scales with 'F' for a friend's view.

Now think of a teacher and how they might rate you. Use a 'T' on each scale.

Choose a member of your family and use a (different) letter to denote their relationship (e.g. D for Dad, M for Mum, B for brother, etc.).

Complete the key at the bottom of the sheet.

PLENARY

Take each scale one at a time. Discuss how individuals have marked how they think a friend, a teacher and their family would rate them. Discuss reasons for the differences.

Who is 'right' about you? Are you a different person to each of them?

UNIT 10: HOW DO OTHERS SEE ME?

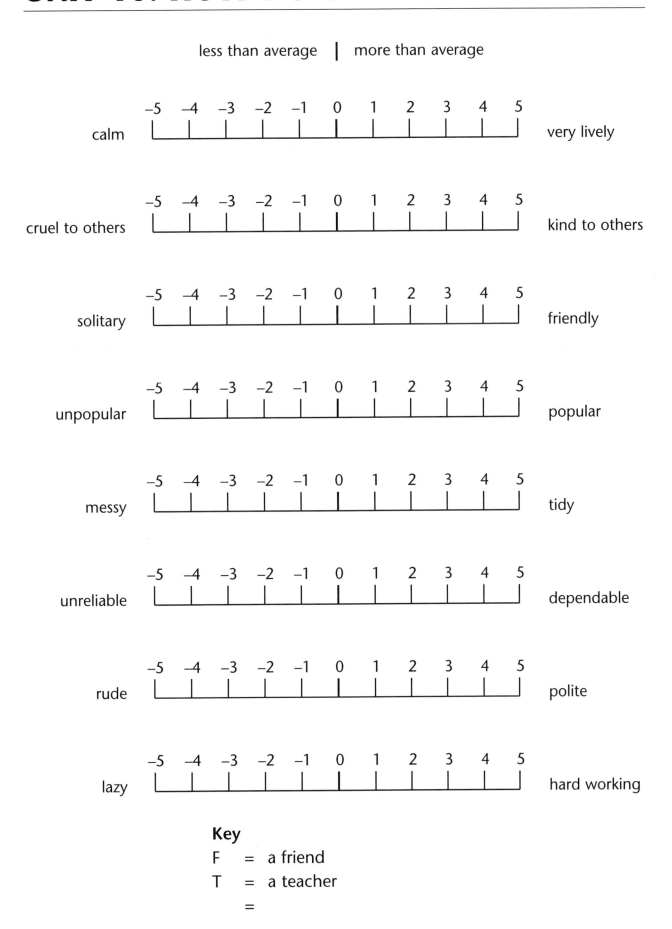

less than average | more than average

	−5 −4 −3 −2 −1 0 1 2 3 4 5	
calm		very lively
cruel to others		kind to others
solitary		friendly
unpopular		popular
messy		tidy
unreliable		dependable
rude		polite
lazy		hard working

Key

F   =   a friend

T   =   a teacher

    =

UNIT 11: INFLUENCES

MAIN FOCUS: LOOKING AT HOW ONE'S LIFE IS INFLUENCED BY OTHERS AND HOW IT AFFECTS OTHERS

Discuss how a young person's life is affected and influenced to different extents by other people. These influences can be positive, negative or both.

Look at the range of suggestions; not all will apply.

On the sheet, draw straight-line arrows from an influence to the 'Me'. Use thin lines for minor influences and thicker lines for people who have a significant influence.

A word or phrase can be written on the arrows to indicate the nature of the influence.

Discuss which influences people have deemed to be minor or significant. Is there a consensus? Is anyone influenced by a celebrity role model?

Now consider how our lives affect other people. In many cases these influences will be reciprocated. Using a different colour, draw arrows from 'Me' to the people whose lives you affect. Again, use a thicker line if the effect is significant. Words or phrases can be used on the arrows.

Share what has been recorded and the thickness of lines used.

PLENARY

Look at the networks that have been drawn. How many are one-way, and how many are reciprocal?

Have some people underestimated or overestimated how their lives are influenced by other people? Has anyone underestimated or overestimated their influence on others?

Are there people whose lives we affect to some degree without realising it?

How can the way we act affect the lives of complete strangers or neighbours?

Is this local, national or global?

Are there positive things we can do to affect the lives of complete strangers (e.g. voluntary work, charity)?

UNIT 11: INFLUENCES

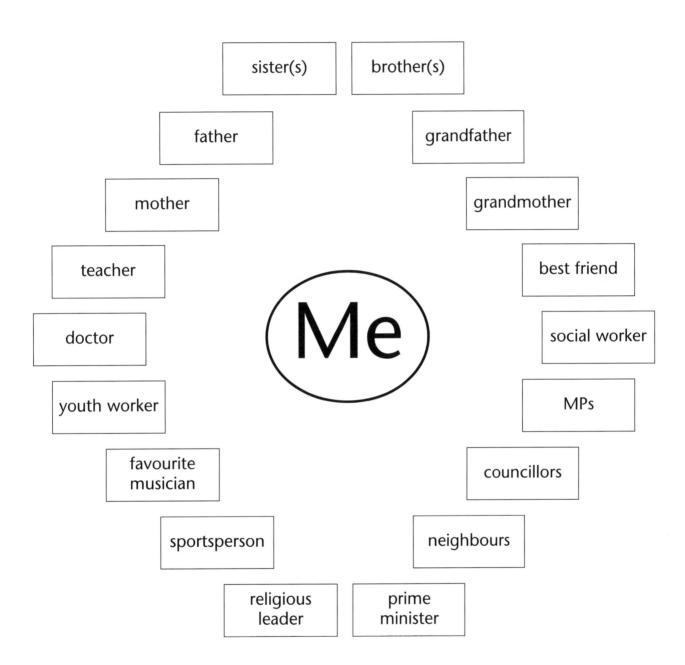

UNIT 12: RELATING TO OTHERS (1)

MAIN FOCUS: HOW ONE RELATES TO OTHER PEOPLE SOCIALLY

This sheet is primarily designed to promote discussion and should be followed up with Unit 13, Relating to others (2).

Each row is intended to be tackled one at a time, marking the scale line only after discussion.

The scale lines represent eight attributes and attitudes relating to other people. The central zero point represents a moderate position.

Look at the first scale line, pointing out that the zero point represents a moderate rating, midway between the two extremes.

For each row clarify the two extreme points and discuss examples of what either end of the scale represents. Discuss any benefits or disadvantages of these extremes – are they 'bad' or 'good'?

1st row – focus on the skill of knowing who one can trust.

2nd row – focus on earning the respect of others.

3rd row – focus on interaction with newcomers.

4th & 5th rows – functional politeness – you don't have to like everyone!

6th row – confidences – focus on not breaking confidences.

7th row – focus on being confident to talk about a problem with someone.

Last row – focus on having trusted people who will encourage and help.

PLENARY

Look at the scale markings of a few volunteers. Do people agree with how they have rated themselves? Give reasons why/why not.

Can people actively change any of theses attributes and attitudes?

Does trust have to be earned?

Does respect have to be earned?

UNIT 12: RELATING TO OTHERS (1)

Put a ✓ where you think you are now.

less than average | more than average

	−5 −4 −3 −2 −1 0 1 2 3 4 5	
I trust anyone		I know who I can trust
I don't care what others think of me		I want people to respect me
I'm shy with strangers		I'm confident with strangers
I only get on well with friends		I can get on well with anyone
I only work well with friends		I can work with anyone
I can't be trusted to keep a secret		I can keep a confidence
I bottle up problems		I share my problems with someone I trust
I have no-one to support me		I have reliable friends who will support me

UNIT 13: RELATING TO OTHERS (2)

MAIN FOCUS: HOW ONE RELATES TO OTHER PEOPLE SOCIALLY

This sheet is primarily designed to promote discussion and should have been preceded by Unit 12, Relating to others (1).

Each row is intended to be tackled one at a time, marking the scale line only after discussion.

The scale lines represent eight attributes and attitudes relating to other people. The central zero point represents a moderate position.

Look at the first scale line, pointing out that the zero point represents a moderate rating, midway between the two extremes.

For each row, clarify the two extreme points and discuss examples of what either end of the scale represents. Discuss any benefits or disadvantages of these extremes – are they 'bad' or 'good'?

1st row – focus on having earned other people's trust.

2nd row – focus on having earned other people's respect.

3rd row – focus on appearing to be friendly and approachable to those you don't know.

4th & 5th rows – focus on your ability to be functionally polite regardless of whether or not you like the other people.

6th row – focus on being trusted by others not to break confidences.

7th row – focus on being seen by others as a reliable person to talk to about a problem.

Last row – focus on having the trust of others to give them.

PLENARY

Look at the scale markings of a few volunteers. Do others agree with how they have rated themselves? Give reasons why/why not.

Can people actively change any of theses attributes and attitudes?

Compare the ratings with those done on sheet 12(1). Have corresponding rows been scored in a similar way?

UNIT 13: RELATING TO OTHERS (2)

Put a ✓ where you think you are now.

less than average | more than average

	–5 –4 –3 –2 –1 0 1 2 3 4 5	
no-one trusts me		everyone can trust me
no-one likes me		everyone respects me
newcomers avoid me		newcomers find me easy to approach
I'm difficult to get on with		people find me easy to get on with
I'm difficult to work with		people find me easy to work with
no-one trusts me to keep a secret		friends confide in me
I'm not a good listener		I'm good at listening to friends with a problem
I don't offer help with problems		friends can rely on me to be supportive

UNIT 14: WHO ARE YOUR FRIENDS?

MAIN FOCUS: DIFFERENTIATING BETWEEN BEST FRIENDS, FRIENDS AND MERE ACQUAINTANCES

What is the difference between an acquaintance and a friend? Arrive at a consensus along the lines of 'An acquaintance is someone you know'; 'A friend is someone whose company you enjoy'.

Look at each of the activities in the oval shapes. Would you do this with an acquaintance; a friend; your best friend?

Use a ruler and three colours to match up the centre mark on the 'acquaintances', 'friends' and 'best friend' boxes to the activities.

PLENARY

Compare the patterns of lines. Which box is linked to most activities?

Are there activities which everyone agrees are not done with acquaintances?

Are there activities that are only done with a best friend?

Are there any activities not linked to best friend?

Can a best friend live miles away and only be contacted by post, telephone and e-mail?

Whose best friend is in school/not in school?

Negotiate definitions of: an acquaintance; friend; best friend.

UNIT 14: WHO ARE YOUR FRIENDS?

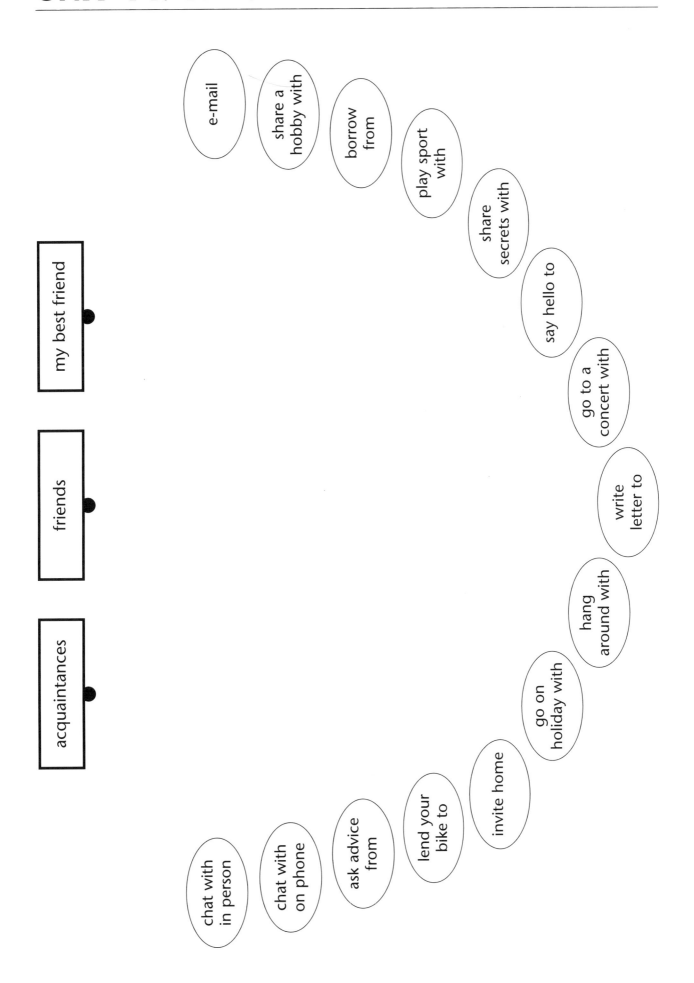

UNIT 15: WHERE ARE YOUR FRIENDS?

MAIN FOCUS: THE VARIETY OF SOCIAL GROUPS AND LOCATIONS FROM WHICH OUR FRIENDS ARE DRAWN

Discuss the range of places from where people have friends – in school; people met on holiday; neighbours; pen friends; friends from synagogue, church, mosque, temple; friends from sports teams, clubs and hobby groups; internet friends.

Match up the figure in the centre of the sheet to the groups in which you have friends.

Can you estimate how many friends you have in each group? Some friends will be in more than one group, so only count them once.

If it helps, use tally marks on the sheet to represent friends you think of.

PLENARY

Does anyone have friends in all of the groups on the sheet?

Who has friends from the most number of groups?

Look at the distribution of your friends across the groups. Do some groups have particularly more friends in them?

Does anyone have friends they've never met (pen friends, internet contacts)?

If you have used sheet 14 look again at what you do with friends. Does each group fit with your idea of a friend or an acquaintance?

UNIT 15: WHERE ARE YOUR FRIENDS?

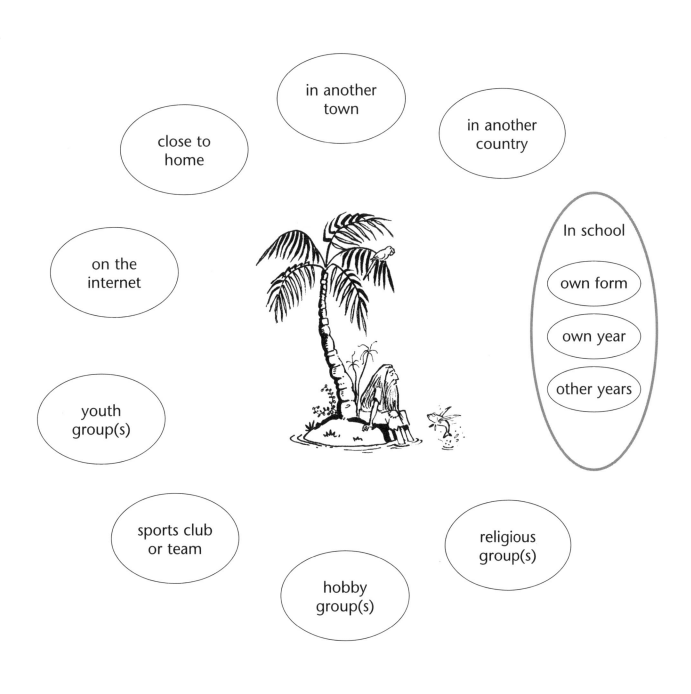

in another town

in another country

close to home

In school

own form

own year

other years

on the internet

youth group(s)

sports club or team

hobby group(s)

religious group(s)

UNIT 16: GOALS

MAIN FOCUS: ASPIRATIONS, AMBITIONS, GOALS

Look at the top section of the sheet. Who would really like to be famous, rich, etc. and why? What are the advantages and disadvantages?

Brainstorm suggestions for the empty box.

Allow time for pupil(s) to highlight any pictures and to do their own illustration and/or comment.

Now look at the middle (career) section of the sheet. Is anyone interested in the careers illustrated? Brainstorm the range of careers that are not illustrated. What are the attractions of different jobs?

Brainstorm suggestions for the empty box.

Allow time for pupil(s) to highlight any pictures and to do their own illustration and/or comment.

Finally, discuss why some people would like (or not like) to aspire to the three illustrations at the bottom.

Brainstorm alternatives for the empty 'achieve' box. Allow time for boxes to be highlighted and completion of the empty box.

PLENARY

Which are important to some/most/all of the group: being rich? famous? a chosen career? having a family? growing old? mattering to someone? being remembered?

Which of these goals can be prepared for (e.g. career choice)?

Which depend upon chance (e.g. meeting 'Mr/Ms Right')?

Which depend upon factors we cannot control (e.g. health)?

UNIT 16: GOALS

What would you like to do?

take life
as it comes

be famous

be rich

be a hero

live where you
want to live

travel the world
for excitement

What would you like to be?

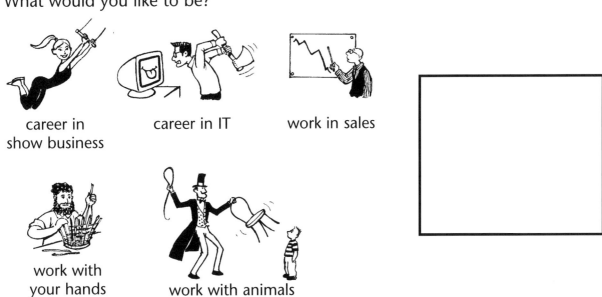

career in
show business

career in IT

work in sales

work with
your hands

work with animals
or children

What would you like to achieve?

  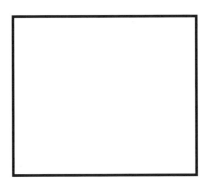

raise a family

grow old

matter to
someone

UNIT 17: AM I BRAVE ENOUGH?

MAIN FOCUS: DISCUSSING DIFFERENT FORMS OF COURAGE, PHYSICAL MENTAL AND MORAL

Introduce, define and illustrate different forms of courage: physical, mental and moral.

Discuss scenarios in which someone's decision would depend on them having, or not having, physical, mental or moral courage.

Discuss if it is brave to put yourself in danger for no real reason. Illustrate with this scenario: friends dare you to join them trespassing on the railway tracks beneath the high-voltage cables, but you know the dangers.

Are your risk-taking friends brave or just stupid?

Discuss which is 'braver', putting yourself needlessly in danger or risking being called 'chicken' by others?

Discuss mental courage such as persistent effort to achieve something; not being pushed into things just to fit in with the crowd.

Discuss moral courage – speaking out for something you believe to be right, or against something you believe to be wrong, when others do not agree.

Look at the examples on the sheet. For each, determine which kind of courage it demonstrates. Invite pupil(s) to highlight the ones they *think* they are brave enough to do.

PLENARY

Everyone has to take decisions that require courage to do, or not do, something.

Taking senseless risks for no reason is not brave, just stupid.

Being brave does not always mean doing something dangerous.

Mental and moral courage can be just as hard as physical courage.

Being yourself and being true to yourself can sometimes require a lot of courage and involve the mental pain of insults, ridicule and isolation.

UNIT 17: AM I BRAVE ENOUGH?

Am I brave enough to:

complain in a shop?

own up to something?

report that I am being bullied?

rescue a cat from a tree?

make my own decisions?

report that my friend is being bullied?

report a crime?

stand up for what I believe to be right?

say what I believe in front of others who might make fun of me?

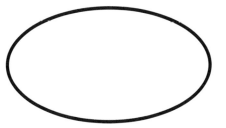

change a baby's nappy?

join a protest march?

walk away from trouble?

always speak the truth?

organise a protest?

say 'No' to doing something I believe to be wrong?

be different?

not follow the 'in crowd'?

take responsibility for my actions?

tell a friend that their 'joke' is offensive?

UNIT 18: WHEN I'M LISTENING/SPEAKING

MAIN FOCUS: WAYS OF SHOWING THAT WE ARE PAYING ATTENTION WHEN SOMEONE IS SPEAKING

Both sheets should be used, sheet (a) then sheet (b).

Sheet (a) Listening

Discuss the importance of good eye contact, demonstrating an unnerving stare and disinterested looks at floor, ceiling, out of window etc. Which do you prefer?

Discuss head movement – non-studio television news interviews often only use one camera and film, the interviewer doing 'continuity nods' in order to edit the interview together. The nods simply mean 'Yes I'm still listening'. Shakes of the head can show disagreement with the speaker or disapproval of what is spoken about.

Continuity words and noises are used to indicate listening, usually by giving reactions to what is said.

We often use a range of facial expressions to give a reaction message without having to interrupt.

Interrupting is sometimes acceptable. Do you explain why you don't agree with something that is said? Does giving a reason make the non-agreement more acceptable?

Sheet (b) Speaking

Do you expect different reactions from others when they are listening to you? How do you expect them to respond?

PLENARY

During conversation the speaker and listener exchange unspoken messages. Most of these contribute to the success of the conversation. The main exception to this is when inappropriate eye contact makes the listener appear disinterested or threatening.

UNIT 18(a): WHEN I'M LISTENING

When I'm listening to someone I:

When someone is speaking I:

never/sometimes/often

interrupt them.

UNIT 18(b): WHEN I'M SPEAKING

When I'm speaking I like the other person to:

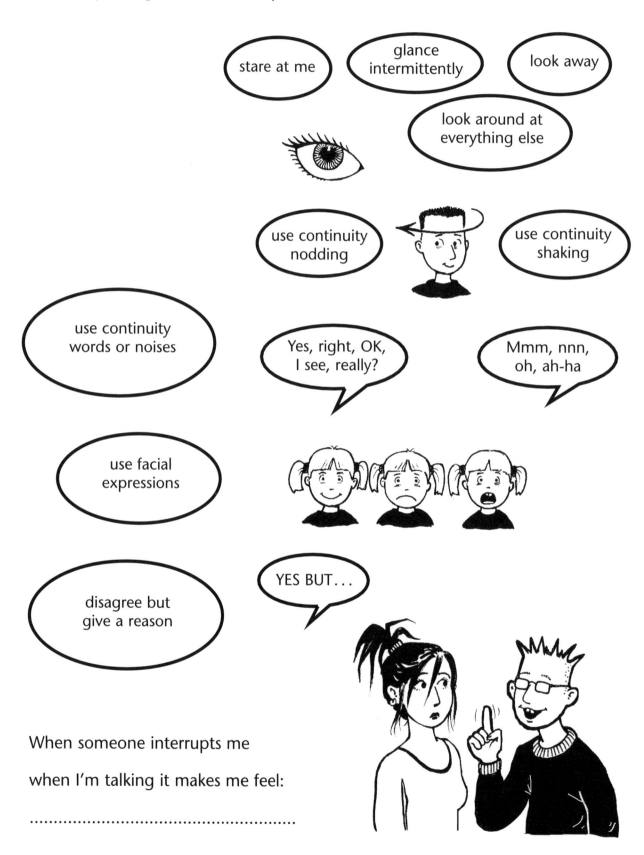

stare at me

glance intermittently

look away

look around at everything else

use continuity nodding

use continuity shaking

use continuity words or noises

Yes, right, OK, I see, really?

Mmm, nnn, oh, ah-ha

use facial expressions

disagree but give a reason

YES BUT...

When someone interrupts me

when I'm talking it makes me feel:

....

UNIT 19: BODY LANGUAGE

MAIN FOCUS: BODY LANGUAGE MESSAGES, BOTH INTENTIONAL AND UNINTENTIONAL

Discuss how the look on our face can give away how we feel. These are unintentional messages and may not always be accurate.

Demonstrate a few exaggerated classroom looks: disinterest, boredom, shock, disgust etc.

Demonstrate how we sometimes deliberately give a non-verbal message by first securing eye contact and using eye and eyebrow movements, shoulder shrugs, head movements etc. The intentional messages may be genuine or false, and may sometimes be meant to be amusing. Invite others to demonstrate.

Brief on how to complete the worksheet.

Complete the eyes and add mouths to the faces in the box to match the label.

Use ruled lines in two colours to match the messages to the unintentional and intentional boxes. Messages can be matched to both. Point out there are two messages involving head shaking. If necessary, demonstrate the difference between a discreet slight shake and one that is very deliberate and exaggerated.

PLENARY

We don't always intend to give the message we are projecting.

The way others interpret these messages can affect their attitude and response to us.

We can use body language to send out messages which could be genuine or false. For example, a genuine smile is brief whereas a false one may last for several seconds.

UNIT 19: BODY LANGUAGE

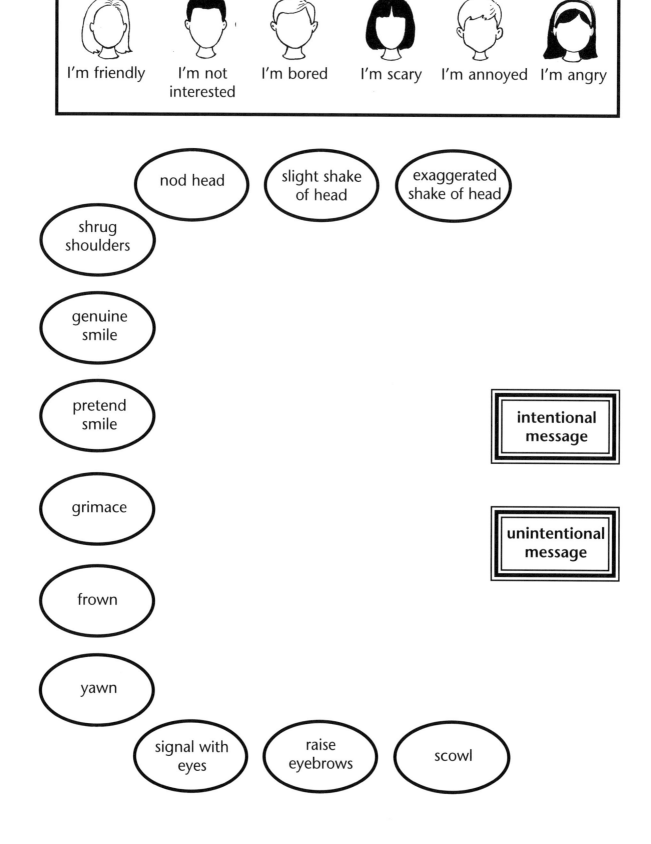

Complete these facial expressions:

I'm friendly   I'm not interested   I'm bored   I'm scary   I'm annoyed   I'm angry

nod head

slight shake of head

exaggerated shake of head

shrug shoulders

genuine smile

pretend smile

intentional message

grimace

unintentional message

frown

yawn

signal with eyes

raise eyebrows

scowl

UNIT 20: PERSONAL SPACE

MAIN FOCUS: PERSONAL SPACE AND PROXIMITY, INVASION OF PERSONAL SPACE

Introduce the notion of personal space. We 'own' the space immediately around us and seek to control who we allow into it.

Look at the zones on the worksheet.

Intimate space – touching or within half a metre of us – is reserved for very close family or partner.

Personal space is strictly limited to close friends and others we allow in for specific purposes (talking to someone, dental visit, queuing). We feel uncomfortable or threatened if someone 'invades' our personal space by being within arm's length of us. Invasion of personal space is more threatening if the 'invader' stands in front of us, face-to-face.

Social space is close enough to socialise informally within a group without invading personal space. Public space is everywhere else.

If working with a group or class, invite a couple of pupils to come out to the front. How close together do they stand? Which space are they in?

Ask them to face each other, to move closer. How do they feel? How would they feel if the other person was a known bully or someone in authority?

On the sheet write suggestions as to who may be allowed in each zone. Avoid names in the intimate zone if you can. Stick to titles such as mum, brother, girlfriend. In other zones names *could* be used.

PLENARY

Physical proximity is related to emotional closeness. We guard, and try to control who comes into, our personal space. If someone comes into our personal space against our wishes, we feel threatened. Aggressive, confrontational people deliberately enter personal space in order to intimidate. Stepping backwards away from an invader *can* reduce the feeling of unease so long as they don't move in close again.

UNIT 20: PERSONAL SPACE

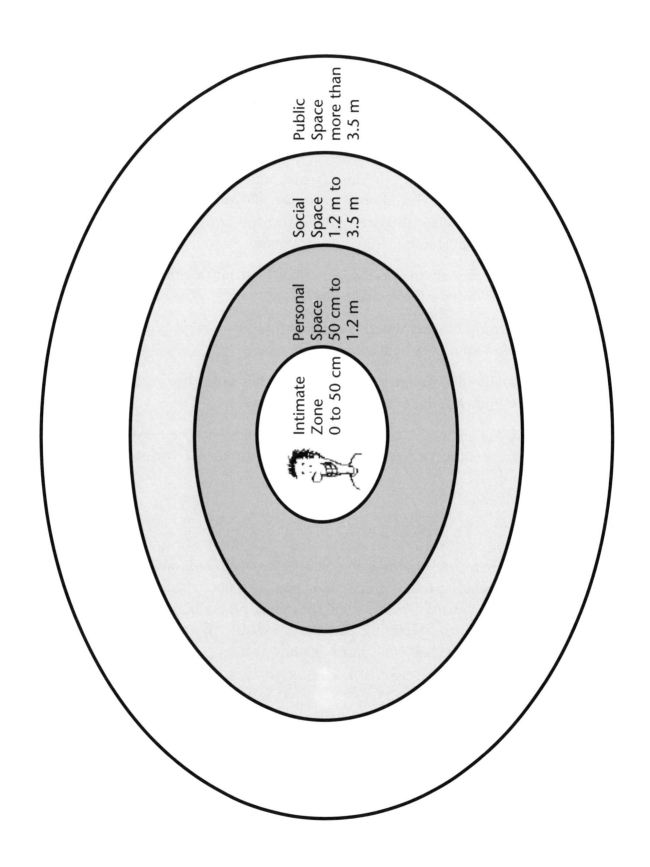

Public
Space
more than
3.5 m

Social
Space
1.2 m to
3.5 m

Personal
Space
50 cm to
1.2 m

Intimate
Zone
0 to 50 cm

UNIT 21: CHOICES GAME

MAIN FOCUS: MAKING APPROPRIATE CHOICES

There is a choice of playing board (B1 and B2) which needs to be blown up to A3 size. Ideally they should be printed on card (two A4 sheets if necessary) and then put together and laminated. There are several sets of Choice cards, three Primary (KS2) and two Secondary (KS 3, 4).

The object of the game is to cross over the centre of the playing board.

Counters can be moved in either direction, and when reaching the centre an exact number is not required.

The Choice cards have scenarios on them and a suggested response.

When a player's counter lands on a highlighted space they pick up the top Choice card from the top of the (face-down and pre-shuffled) pile. The card is read out and the players have to decide (voting if necessary) if the response is a 'good' choice or not. Some choice card responses are, intentionally, metaphorically 'grey' rather than black-and-white.

If it is a 'good' choice the player is either promoted inwards instead of remaining on the same level, or else remains on the same level instead of being demoted outwards.

If working one to one, both you and the pupil should play with two counters each, deciding which one to move when you have thrown the dice.

PLENARY

Who won each game?

Were there times when a vote was needed because the players were not unanimous about the response on a card? Which card(s) caused the debate?

Is there always a 'good' and a 'bad' choice, or is it sometimes a matter of making a 'better' or 'less bad' decision?

CHOICES GAME B1

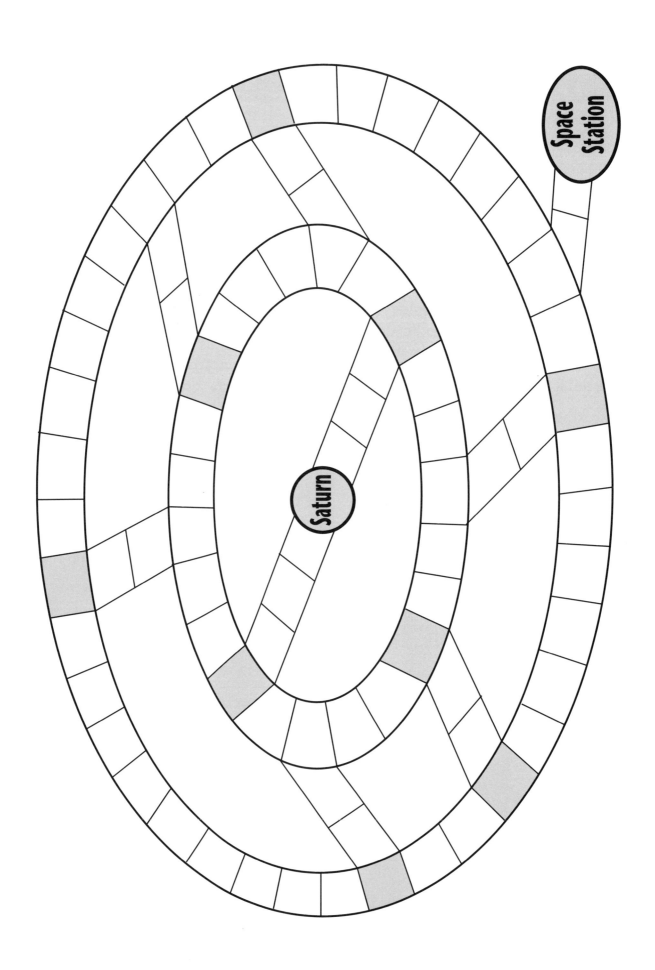

CHOICES GAME B2

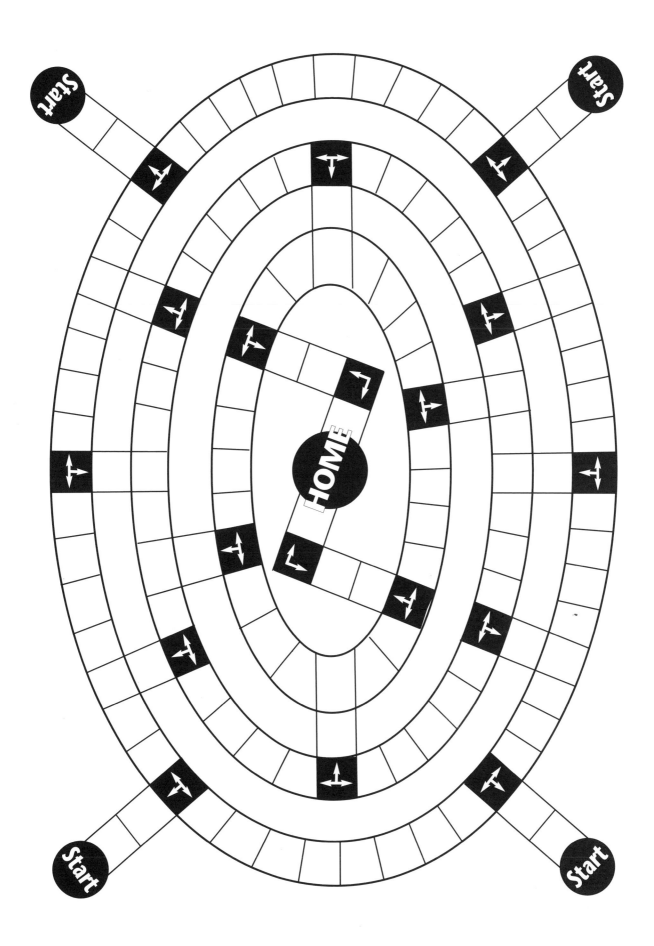

CHOICES GAME: PRIMARY CHOICE CARDS 1

A boy or girl pushes past you. You ignore it.	A boy or girl pushes past you. You apologise for being in *their* way.	A boy or girl pushes past you. You push them back.
A boy or girl pushes past you. You shout at them.	Someone pushes into the line in front of you. You hit them.	Someone pushes into the line in front of you. You tell them to go to the back.
Someone pushes into the line in front of you. You tell a teacher or supervisor.	Someone pushes into the line in front of you. You let them stay in front of you.	Someone calls you 'Big Ears'. You call them something nasty.
Someone calls you 'Big Ears'. You hit them.	Someone calls you 'Big Ears'. You say, 'Yes they are great for listening!'	Someone who isn't a friend joins in the game you're playing. You let them.
Someone who isn't a friend joins in the game you're playing. You let them, and tell them the rules.	Someone who isn't a friend joins in the game you're playing. You tell them to go away.	Someone who isn't a friend joins in the game you're playing. You tell your family when you go home.

CHOICES GAME: PRIMARY CHOICE CARDS 2

Someone joins in the game you're playing. You tell them to go away and not spoil the game.	Someone joins in the game you're playing. You help them to join in.	Someone joins in the game you're playing. You push them away.
You are talking to your teacher and someone joins in. You push them away.	You are talking to your teacher and someone joins in. You let them join in.	You are talking to your teacher and someone joins in. You ask them to wait.
You are talking to your teacher and someone joins in. You complain.	You are talking to a friend and someone interrupts. You tell them to go away.	You are talking to a friend and someone interrupts. You let them join in.
You are talking to a friend and someone interrupts. You push them away.	Someone hits you. You push them away.	Someone hits you. You hit them back.
Someone hits you. You do nothing about it.	Someone hits you. You tell a teacher or dinner supervisor.	Someone hits you. You ask someone else to hit them back for you.

CHOICES GAME: PRIMARY CHOICE CARDS 3

Someone kicks your friend. **You tell your friend to kick them back.**	Someone kicks your friend. You tell a member of staff.	Someone kicks your friend. **You** kick or hit the person back.
Someone is noisy in class and won't let you get on with your work. You try to ignore them.	Someone is noisy in class and won't let you get on with your work. You ask them to shut up.	Someone is noisy in class and won't let you get on with your work. You shout at them to shut up.
Someone is noisy in class and won't let you get on with your work. You complain to your teacher.	Someone else has left a mess on your table. You complain to your teacher.	Someone else has left a mess on your table. You clear it up yourself.
Someone else has left a mess on your table. You tell them to clear it up.	Someone else has left a mess on your table. You move the mess and put it on their table.	Someone else has left a mess on your table. You ask them to clear it up.
Someone else has left a mess on your table. You leave the mess where it is on your table.		

CHOICES GAME: SECONDARY CHOICE CARDS 1

Another student pushes past you. You ignore them.	Another student pushes past you. You apologise for being in *their* way!	Another student pushes past you. You push them back.
Another student pushes past you. You shout at them.	Another student pushes in front of you in the dinner queue. You shout at them.	Another student pushes in front of you in the dinner queue. You tell them to go to the back.
Another student pushes in front of you in the dinner queue. You push them away.	Another student pushes in front of you in the dinner queue. You let them stay in front of you.	Someone calls you 'Big Ears'. You say, 'Yes they are great for listening'
Someone calls you 'Big Ears'. You hit them.	Someone calls you 'Big Ears'. You ignore it or pretend you didn't hear them.	Someone calls you 'Big Ears'. You insult them back.
You are talking to a teacher and someone joins in. You let them join in.	You are talking to a teacher and someone joins in. You ask them to wait till you've finished.	It's the end of a lesson and someone has left a mess on your table. You leave the mess for the next class.

CHOICES GAME: SECONDARY CHOICE CARDS 2

You are talking to a friend and someone interrupts. You tell them to go away.	You are talking to a friend and someone interrupts. You let them join in.	Someone you don't like insults you. You ignore them because 'they're not worth it'.
Someone you don't like insults you. You laugh.	Someone you don't like insults you. You push them away or hit them.	Someone you don't like insults you. You insult them back.
Someone hits you. You do nothing about it.	Someone hits you. You report it.	Someone hits you. You hit them back.
Someone is noisy in a lesson and won't let you get on with your work. You try to ignore them.	Someone is noisy in a lesson and won't let you get on with your work. You ask them to keep quiet.	Someone is noisy in a lesson and won't let you get on with your work. You **shout** at them to shut up.
Someone is noisy in a lesson and won't let you get on with your work. You complain to the teacher.	It's the end of a lesson and someone has left a mess on your table. You ask them to clear it up.	It's the end of a lesson and someone has left a mess on your table. You clear it up.

UNIT 22: INTERACTION

MAIN FOCUS: WHO CAN WE INTERACT AND/OR WORK WITH – CAN WE GET ON WITH OTHERS WITHOUT HAVING TO LIKE THEM?

Discuss a range of feelings towards other people, from loathing to liking, including indifference (as with total strangers). Raise the point that we can respect people without necessarily liking or disliking them. (For example, rivals in sport often respect their opponents because of their level of skill and dedication.)

Talk through different levels of interaction ranging from a grudgingly grunted 'Hello' through to friendly, informal chat about holidays, family etc.

Discuss being able to work with people as partners or team members. Do you have to like people to be functionally polite?

Introduce the worksheet and its two columns. The person categories on the left should be looked at one at a time and matched up with ruled lines to the appropriate levels of interaction on the right. Different colours and styles of line can be used for increased clarity.

PLENARY

Go through the links of a few people and compare their responses with those of others. Discuss where there is consensus or disagreement.

Who can work with practically anyone?

Do you have to like or respect someone to get along with them politely?

Do you have to like or respect someone to work with them?

How important is being functionally polite to people we don't know or people we don't particularly like or respect?

Does functional politeness help in work or social situations?

Confess to the group! While you are able to work with the rest of the staff, do you really like all of them?

UNIT 22: INTERACTION

people I like

people I don't like

people I don't know very well

people I respect

friends

family

some teachers

most teachers

total strangers

speak to

chat with

joke with

be polite to

be pleasant with

be friendly with

give help to

work in a pair with

work in a team with

UNIT 23: WHO MAKES YOU ANGRY?

MAIN FOCUS: RELIEVING PENT-UP ANGER AND AGGRESSION

THESE SHEETS MUST ONLY BE USED IN A ONE TO ONE SITUATION. GIVE CAREFUL CONSIDERATION TO WHETHER OR NOT EITHER SHEET IS APPROPRIATE FOR THE INDIVIDUAL PUPIL CONCERNED.

The pupil must understand that the contents of each sheet are pretend, and should be approached with some humour.

These sheets are intended to release pent-up anger and frustration in a safe environment so that it is not directed at the person who is the object of the anger.

Sheet 23(a) needs to be blown up to A3 size.

Sheet 23(b) needs to be photocopied onto A4 card.

At the very start, both you and the pupil must make an agreement not to tell anyone about the sheet(s) or contents. If you feel the pupil cannot keep this confidence DO NOT USE THEM.

The pupil needs to be guided through it stage by stage, maintaining an atmosphere of (albeit black) humour.

Make it very clear that the sheet is pretend.

At the end, the sheet should be completely destroyed.

PLENARY

Stress that taking out pent-up aggression against paper or other inanimate objects is better than losing your temper.

Losing your temper is losing your control. Losing your control leaves you powerless.

UNIT 23(a): WHO MAKES YOU ANGRY?

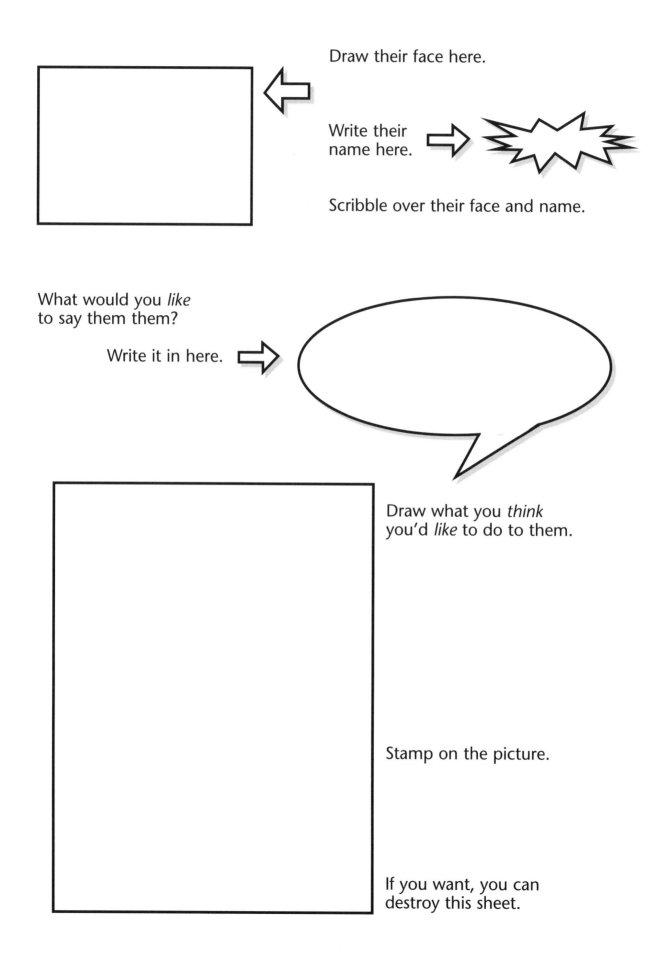

Draw their face here.

Write their name here.

Scribble over their face and name.

What would you *like* to say them them?

Write it in here.

Draw what you *think* you'd *like* to do to them.

Stamp on the picture.

If you want, you can destroy this sheet.

UNIT 23(b): THINK OF WHO *REALLY* MAKES YOU ANGRY

Colour this head above the broken line so that it looks like them.

Cut off the picture below and colour the crocodiles.

Draw nasty slimy things floating in the lake.

Cut slits along the broken lines.

Slide the strip through the top slit and out through the bottom slit.

Wiggle the end of the strip to make the person struggle in the slimy crocodile pool.

Cut this out with the head and arms attached.

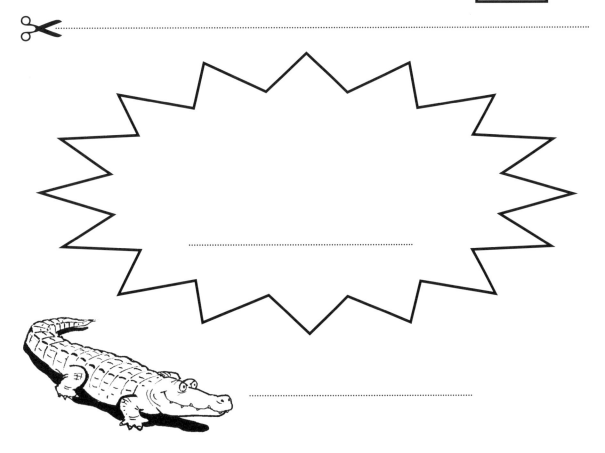

UNIT 24: LISTEN TO YOUR BODY

MAIN FOCUS: RECOGNISING THE PHYSICAL INDICATORS AS A STATE OF MILD ANNOYANCE BUILDS UP INTO ANGER

Look at the first illustration on the page – clearly someone who is a little tense and irritated. How can we tell from the picture?

Talk through the list of tell-tale signs which may indicate rising levels of frustration or annoyance.

You can relate most of these to the 'fight or flight' response of our caveman ancestors, as their brains prepared them for physical exertion (fighting or running away) by increasing oxygen intake through faster breathing and pulse, and directing it to muscles.

Although cavemen never drove cars, drivers today often tense their hands on the steering wheel when they become stressed while driving or stuck in traffic jams over which they have no control.

Discuss which physical signs pupils recognise in themselves. If working one to one discuss your own anger indicators.

Are there any signs not listed that people recognise in themselves when they are becoming angry?

Allow time for the sheet to be completed, including adding any extra signs. Point out the importance of answering the question at the bottom.

PLENARY

It takes time for anger to build up.

Frustration at one situation can be carried over into another (e.g. an incident in one lesson might make someone shorter-tempered).

If we recognise the danger signs of rising anger we have the power to prevent it from escalating into an uncontrolled eruption.

UNIT 24: LISTEN TO YOUR BODY

Listen to what your body is telling you!

Anger doesn't just 'happen'; there are warning signs to watch for.

When you are becoming angry,

	Yes	No
do you feel hot?	☐	☐
does your face go red?	☐	☐
does your heart beat faster?	☐	☐
do you breathe faster?	☐	☐
do you feel breathless?	☐	☐
do you get a feeling in your stomach?	☐	☐
do your hands feel hot and sweaty?	☐	☐
do you clench your fists?	☐	☐
do your muscles tense?	☐	☐
does your mouth feel dry?	☐	☐
do you feel worried, tense, unsure?	☐	☐
....	☐	
....	☐	

When you feel anger building up, what do you do?

....

UNIT 25: DEALING WITH CONFLICT (1)

MAIN FOCUS: DISCUSSING DIFFERENT WAYS OF RESOLVING A CONFLICT SITUATION

Discuss the range of seriousness of possible conflict situations, ranging from two nursery children wanting to play with the same toy through to road rage and even war. Briefly bring in causes for some wars – religious intolerance, grabbing natural resources, and the 'War of Jenkins' Ear' (1739, declared after English sea captain Robert Jenkins was captured, tortured and mutilated by the Spanish).

Look through the four proposed responses to conflicts and encourage debate on the advantages and disadvantages of each.

Give in – does this mean loss of face or simply showing that you are more grown up?

Be confrontational – does this avoid loss of face? Will someone have to back down?

Seek arbitration – is this giving up and telling tales or a sign that you're acting sensibly in seeking a fair settlement?

Negotiate – can both parties really be partial winners?

Allow time for pupils to complete the boxes, pointing out that some boxes may need to be left empty. Ask for suggestions of the types of people these solutions might work with, without naming names.

PLENARY

There is no 'fits all' solution.

Giving in/walking away could either lose or gain you respect depending upon the circumstances.

Being confrontational makes a bad situation worse and eventually one side may have to back down to stop the conflict.

Negotiation works if both sides feel they have gained something, though not everything.

UNIT 25: DEALING WITH CONFLICT (1)

Give in/walk away Let them have their own way because it really isn't worth the hassle. 	☺ **Good Points** ☹ **Bad Points** **Who *might* it work with?**
Be confrontational Be aggressive –  shout and insult the other person. Ignore what they say or shout.	☺ **Good points** ☹ **Bad points** **Who *might* it work with?**
Seek arbitration Agree to ask someone else, such as a teacher or parent, to sort things out. 	☺ **Good points** ☹ **Bad points** **Who *might* it work with?**
Negotiate Suggest a solution which has *some* benefit for both of you. Discuss it and come to an agreement. 	☺ **Good points** ☹ **Bad points** **Who *might* it work with?**

UNIT 26: DEALING WITH CONFLICT (2)

MAIN FOCUS: APPLYING DIFFERENT WAYS OF RESOLVING A CONFLICT SITUATION

This sheet is intended to be used after sheet 25.

Recap on the four suggested approaches to conflict situations on sheet 25.

Look at the first scenario. Take each approach in turn and discuss what would happen if it was used in this situation. Would it resolve the problem? What would it 'cost' both parties? Would there be a loser? Which would be the easiest solution?

Allow time for pupils to discuss and complete both scenarios.

Share the views that some have put down.

If time allows, you could discuss a third scenario suggested by a pupil.

PLENARY

In the first scenario, the confrontational approach doesn't work. The shouting just drowns out the programme you are trying to watch. It is quicker to fetch the stuff. Involving a third party or negotiating will also lose you precious minutes of your programme.

In the second scenario, confrontation is likely to cause bad feeling and damage team spirit. It might also get one or both of you kicked out.

Asking a team coach to arbitrate might work, but might leave behind ill feeling. Negotiation could involve either sharing responsibility or agreeing to have a secret ballot of the team members.

UNIT 26: DEALING WITH CONFLICT (2)

Situation 1

You are watching your favourite programme. Your older brother/sister demands that you fetch and return the things you 'borrowed' (without asking) NOW!

Give in	Be confrontational
Seek arbitration	**Negotiate**

Situation 2

You think that you should captain a sports team because you are the best. Another member of the team says they are the best and should be captain.

Give in	Be confrontational
Seek arbitration	**Negotiate**

UNIT 27: WHY DID THEY DO THAT?

MAIN FOCUS: NOT JUMPING TO CONCLUSIONS ABOUT WHY PEOPLE DO THINGS THAT AFFECT US

Have a brief look at the first scenario on the sheet and brainstorm possibilities. Is the friend just absent-minded? Are they hurrying because they're late? Are they preoccupied or upset by some bad news? Are they thinking about or planning something as they walk? Do they genuinely not see you because of the fast-moving crush in the corridor?

Throw in the possibility that perhaps for some unknown reason they wanted to deliberately upset you.

Give a brief overview of the other scenarios. Is the bumping accidental (easy with busy, bustling corridors) or deliberate? Do teachers share jobs or choose someone for other reasons? Does your best friend really want to upset you?

Allow discussion in pairs. Ask for three different, single-sentence, innocent reasons why the incident may have happened.

PLENARY

Share some people's suggestions of innocent reasons behind each scenario.

It's no use trying to guess or make up why we think someone did something – if they don't tell us, we don't know the real reason.

Some people jump to the wrong conclusion and assume that offence was intended.

Most people don't do things intended to annoy or upset others.

UNIT 27: WHY DID THEY DO THAT?

People sometimes upset or annoy us without meaning to. There may be reasons we don't know about.

Give three reasons why each of these *might* have happened.

A friend walks
straight past
you without
speaking.

....

....

....

Someone
bumps into
you in the
corridor.

....

....

....

A teacher
chooses
someone else
to do a job.

....

....

....

Your best
friend is
sitting by
someone else.

....

....

....

UNIT 28: WHICH BUTTONS SET YOU OFF?

MAIN FOCUS: IDENTIFYING ONE'S OWN PERSONAL ANGER TRIGGERS

Do not give out the worksheet at the beginning.

Pretend that you have a remote control and role-play using it to control a 'safe' member of the group.

Introduce the analogy that sometimes imaginary remote controls can be used to make people react in a negative way – they 'set you off'.

Now hand out the remote control worksheets.

Which buttons set you off? Look through the buttons on the sheet and ask who is set off by each. Share one or two of your own buttons.

Allow time for discussion and for people to colour the buttons that affect them.

Fill in the empty button labels.

PLENARY

On a television or video remote control there are usually some buttons that don't appear to do anything. We soon learn not to bother pressing those. We quickly identify the buttons that do make something happen. If we react badly to a particular button being pressed it is sure to be used again and again.

If we are able to suppress a negative reaction the person who presses it will give up trying that button on you, though it may take some time.

UNIT 28: WHICH BUTTONS SET YOU OFF?

being called names	someone insulting my family	someone insulting my friends	being talked about behind my back	being shouted at
being treated unfairly	being called a liar	being pushed or jostled	not being given a chance	being blamed unfairly
getting work wrong	making mistakes	being interrupted when I'm talking	being told off for what I've done	being told off for what I haven't done
people not listening to what I'm trying to say	being ignored	someone taking my things	someone breaking my things	people disturbing me when I'm working

Add new buttons.

What else sets you off?

UNIT 29: BLOCKING THE SIGNAL

MAIN FOCUS: STRATEGIES TO DEAL WITH ATTEMPTS BY OTHERS TO MANIPULATE YOUR OWN PERSONAL ANGER TRIGGERS

This sheet is intended to be used as a follow-up to 28.

Refer back to the buttons on sheet 28 and don't yet give out sheet 29. Recap on the analogy of a television remote control being used by someone else to make you react negatively. What happens if someone is standing between the TV and the control when you try to use it? The signal is blocked.

Apply this to the analogy – if you can block the signal when someone tries to wind you up, then that wind-up doesn't work.

Now distribute 29. Look through the suggested strategies and expand on each.

Which are more difficult to do?

Which can you do without the other person knowing?

Which are clear for all to see (and hear)?

Who has tried these strategies?

Are there other positive strategies which work?

PLENARY

Some signal-blocking strategies are more effective for some people than for others. Some may not work straight away but rely on the other person to get bored, with no visible reaction to their goading.

Some strategies rely upon controlling your physical and/or emotional responses, while others provide an outlet to release the annoyance.

Pretending not to be affected by hurtful things can still be painful.

If you react in a negative way the goader has 'won' because they have caused you to react.

UNIT 29: BLOCKING THE SIGNAL

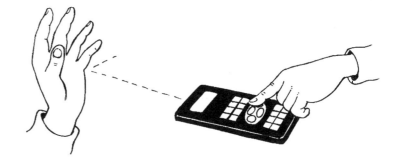

Remote controls
don't work if you
block out the signal.

Here are some ways to *block the anger signal.*
Tick the ones you use and ones you might try.
Add some methods of your own.

	I do this:	I'll try this:
walk away	☐	☐
count in your head	☐	☐
count out loud	☐	☐
breathe slowly	☐	☐
relax your tensed muscles	☐	☐
talk yourself into calming down	☐	☐
imagine the person doing something else	☐	☐
pretend you're not bothered	☐	☐
pretend you're somewhere else	☐	☐
simply ignore it	☐	☐
do something else	☐	☐
listen to music	☐	☐
go somewhere 'safe'	☐	☐
hit, break or throw something	☐	☐
do something energetic	☐	☐
....	☐	
....	☐	
....	☐	

UNIT 30: USE YOUR ANGER

MAIN FOCUS: USING DIRECTED AND CONTROLLED ANGER AS A MOTIVATOR

Everyone gets angry, but many people are able to hide it.

Anger is best directed at an issue, or situation, rather than at a person who represents it.

Controlled anger is a great motivator – refer to social reformers who won us the vote, brought an end to slavery and child labour, etc.

Look at the sheet. Here are some ground rules for directing our anger at a problem. Discuss and elaborate on the importance of each. Demonstrate quiet, slow, but firm, speech.

Stress the importance of being in control of oneself.

What reaction would being abusive have on the other person?

Some problems will not be solved until someone is *prepared* to solve them instead of escalating the situation.

Discuss the warning signs on the sheet.

Ask them to design their own warning sign, picture and caption.

PLENARY

Negative anger puts us out of our own control.

Anger can motivate us to do something, either negative (as in taking revenge) or positive, by solving the problem.

Directing controlled anger at a problem can help us to find a solution instead of an escalation.

Looking for or offering a solution is a sign of maturity.

UNIT 30: USE YOUR ANGER

Anger *can* be useful **if it is controlled.**
Anger can *motivate* people to take positive action, to solve a problem.

You must:

Don't shout

- ☺ stay calm
- ☺ talk quietly, slowly but firmly
- ☺ be assertive
- ☺ say what has upset or offended you
- ☺ treat the other person with respect
- ☺ listen to their side
- ☺ be prepared to reach an agreement

Find a good way out

You mustn't:

Don't lose self-control

- ☹ blame the other person
- ☹ use insults
- ☹ mock the other person
- ☹ use bad language
- ☹ exaggerate
- ☹ be confrontational

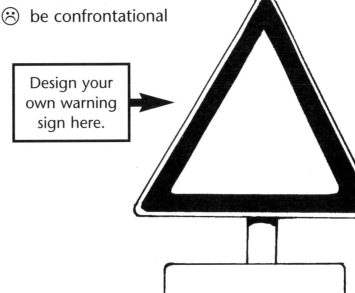

Beware of insults

Design your own warning sign here.

Compromise Zone

A solution needs both sides to agree.

UNIT 31: WHO'S IN CONTROL?

MAIN FOCUS: WHO INFLUENCES OUR ACTIONS? WHO IS AFFECTED BY WHAT WE DO?

The worksheet is divided into two sections: the upper half concerned with deciding what we do and the lower concerned with the consequences. Tackle these two sections one at a time.

Upper section

Make a clear distinction between people who tell us what to do and those who have power or authority to make us do things.

Pose a few questions such as:

'Who decides that you . . .   . . . must come to school?'
. . . must go to the dentist?'
. . . are too ill to leave the house?'
. . . need new trainers?'

Allow time for the two question boxes to be matched up to the people and organisations.

Lower section

Point out that the credit and blame boxes are likely to be only connected to those who exercise authority over us. The remaining box could include more general groups such as society.

Allow discussion as the lower boxes are matched up to the central section.

Look at the pattern. Discuss and compare who has matched what to what. Which of the ovals has the most matches?

PLENARY

'Myself' is likely to be matched to all five questions.

While people who have authority can tell us what to do, we are required to do it.

Many people can benefit from the good things we do, but many could suffer if we do bad things.

We are the people who are most affected by the benefits or consequences of what we do.

UNIT 31: WHO'S IN CONTROL?

Who controls what you do?

Who tells you what to do?

the police

my school

my friends

my family

myself

society

the council

the government

Who gets the benefit or suffers the consequences?

Who gets the blame for the bad things?

Who gets the credit for the good things?

UNIT 32: HOW ANNOYING!

MAIN FOCUS: LOOKING AT THE RANGE OF ANNOYANCE AND DIFFERENTIATING BETWEEN BEING ANNOYED, ANGRY OR FURIOUS

Brainstorm words to describe being irritated, annoyed, miffed etc., including colloquial expressions. Group those that are felt to be of equal seriousness and attempt to rank them all, from least serious to most serious.

Discuss the potential sources of annoyance on the sheet. On the scale of 1 to 5 where would people place them? Who agrees/disagrees? Compare your view with the consensus.

Ask everyone (include yourself, if you like) to insert three potential sources of annoyance in the three boxes before linking each potential annoyance with a point on the scale. Ensure that they become progressively more annoying, left to right.

PLENARY

Different stimuli have different effects on all of us, due partly to what offends us, how tolerant we are and how much we choose to ignore.

Little things can become increasingly irritating as time progresses.

There is a big difference between something that irritates and something that annoys, angers or infuriates.

UNIT 32: HOW ANNOYING!

| people dropping litter | people chewing with mouth open | people picking on you | people dumping rubbish |

| automated telephone answering | people picking on others | queue jumpers | being pushed or jostled |

| being called names | adverts | verbal bullying | physical bullying |

no effect	**irritated**	**annoyed**	**angry**	**furious**
1	**2**	**3**	**4**	**5**

| someone constantly saying 'actually' or 'actual' | poor service from a shop | someone constantly tapping their fingers |

| being judged by what you wear | someone constantly swearing | adults moaning about 'young people today' |

| sexual discrimination | sexist jokes | racist jokes | racial discrimination |

UNIT 33: PEER PRESSURE

MAIN FOCUS: WAYS OF RESISTING PEER PRESSURE

Clarify that everyone understands the terms 'peer' and 'peer pressure'.

Exchange examples of things that others have tried to get us to do to prove we're not 'chicken' – include stupid risks and things we believe to be wrong (crime, organised bullying etc.).

Look at the responses used on sheet 33(a) and discuss what sorts of comments they are – are they jokey, assertive, alternative suggestions, compliments, reasons not to etc.?

Would some responses result in losing face? Would any result in the loss of friends? Do you really want 'friends' who would get you into danger or trouble? Could they result in you being regarded as more mature or sensible?

Return to the scenarios already shared. Which suggested responses might work?

Now use sheet 33(b) to make alternative responses. Encourage use of humour, assertiveness and distracting away from the suggestion with something more sensible.

PLENARY

Some peers (make a distinction between peers and genuine friends) will pressure others to do things as a way of exercising power and control over them.

Everyone is responsible for what they do – it's no use trying to blame someone else.

Taking your own decisions could keep you out of trouble.

Risk without a purpose (e.g. rescue) is pointless and stupid.

Suggesting a sensible alternative is a positive way of side-stepping a stupid suggestion.

UNIT 33(a): PEER PRESSURE

UNIT 33(b): PEER PRESSURE

Imagine that a 'friend' has told you to do something risky or something you feel is wrong.

Look at the responses on sheet 33 (a) and make some similar ones of your own.

UNIT 34: CRANKING UP THE ANGER

MAIN FOCUS: INTRODUCING THE NOTION THAT CONFRONTATIONS ARE USUALLY THE RESULT OF AN ESCALATING CHAIN OF ACTIONS AND REACTIONS INVOLVING AT LEAST TWO PARTIES

Starting with the first chain link (top left) start to go through the events in this scenario. After the first three links discuss: 'Is there an innocent party?' 'Is there a guilty party?'

Continue through to the thirteenth link ('Fred does the same') and ask again if there is clearly one guilty and one innocent party.

What initially upset the other driver? Had he any reason to be upset? What did the other driver do to crank up the anger?

Discuss Fred's part – have his reactions cranked up the anger of the other driver?

Speculate, briefly, how the scenario might have ended – agreement? violence? injury? police? prosecution? legal consequences?

Look at the chain again. Mark where the chain could have been broken by one of the two parties not reacting.

Should we blame the gorilla-like driver completely?

Should Fred, presumably a reasonable and sensible person, take any of the blame?

PLENARY

As anger gets cranked up, people often revert to instinctive, caveman-like behaviour instead of using their intelligence.

Getting stressed up over trivia such as being overtaken isn't good for mental or physical wellbeing.

Both parties in this scenario could suffer consequences such as injury, car damage, a fine, driving ban, imprisonment etc.

Using your twenty-first-century brain and saying 'It's not worth the hassle' beats being a caveman.

UNIT 34: CRANKING UP THE ANGER

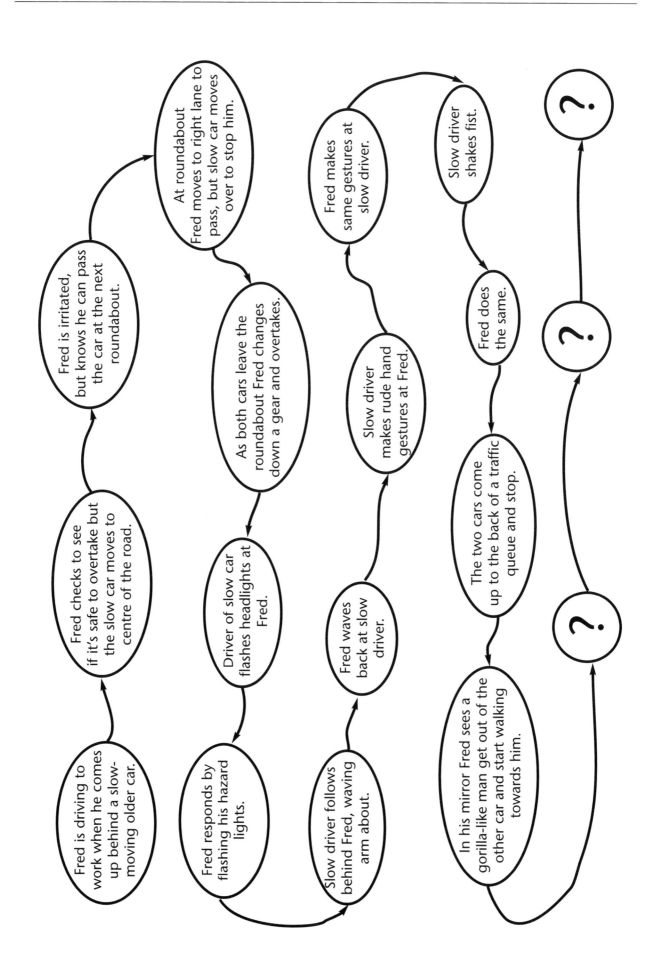

Fred is driving to work when he comes up behind a slow-moving older car.

Fred checks to see if it's safe to overtake but the slow car moves to centre of the road.

Fred is irritated, but knows he can pass the car at the next roundabout.

At roundabout Fred moves to right lane to pass, but slow car moves over to stop him.

As both cars leave the roundabout Fred changes down a gear and overtakes.

Driver of slow car flashes headlights at Fred.

Fred responds by flashing his hazard lights.

Slow driver follows behind Fred, waving arm about.

Fred waves back at slow driver.

Slow driver makes rude hand gestures at Fred.

Fred makes same gestures at slow driver.

Slow driver shakes fist.

Fred does the same.

The two cars come up to the back of a traffic queue and stop.

In his mirror Fred sees a gorilla-like man get out of the other car and start walking towards him.

?   ?   ?

UNIT 35: BACK-TRACKING

MAIN FOCUS: BACK-TRACKING THROUGH THE ANTECEDENTS TO AN INCIDENT TO IDENTIFY WHERE THE ESCALATING CHAIN OF EVENTS COULD HAVE BEEN BROKEN

This sheet is intended to follow sheet 33; however, it can be used on its own with an appropriate preamble.

Look at the link which has text in it and establish that the incident described is a serious one involving two young people totally not in control of their actions, and which would have taken several members of staff to prevent.

Discuss what might have triggered the actual fight (i.e. both parties assaulting each other). Discuss what might have been the trigger.

Introduce the technique of back-tracking, looking at what was the trigger for each stage of the escalation.

Pupils can work individually or in pairs to complete the chain of events backwards.

Share a few of the scenarios forwards, looking at points where the chain of events could have been broken by one party deciding to act differently.

Allow pupils a few minutes to think about and insert possible consequences of the main incident.

PLENARY

Back-tracking from a real incident helps to identify the initial cause and bad choices that fuelled the escalation. Looking at alternative choices and actions could help us prevent a potential problem escalating out of control.

It is important to be in control of what you do and say.

Making wrong choices can lead to actions we regret and consequences we don't want.

UNIT 35: BACK-TRACKING

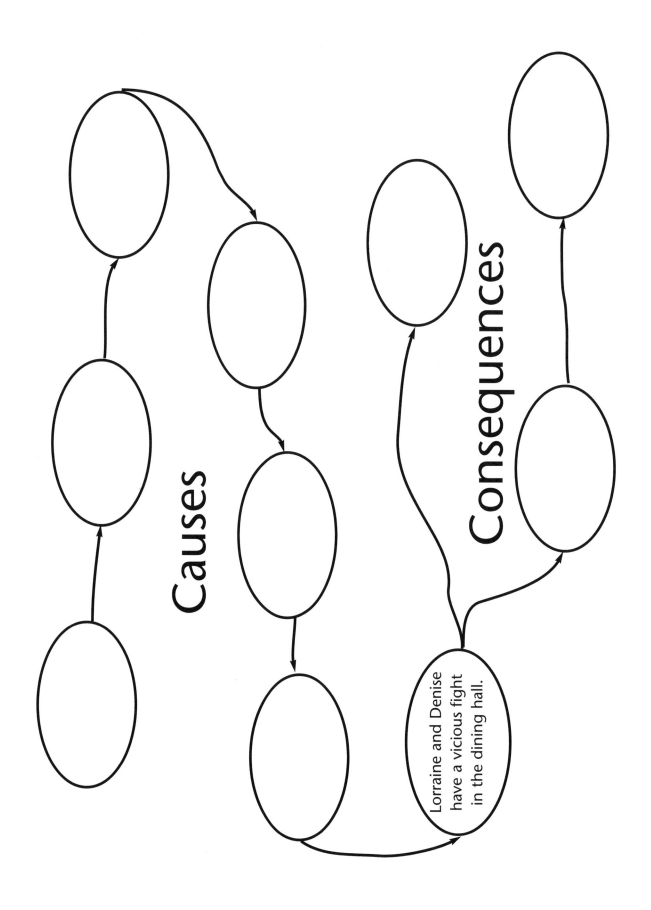

Causes

Consequences

Lorraine and Denise have a vicious fight in the dining hall.

UNIT 36: CHAIN BREAKERS

MAIN FOCUS: LOOKING AT A SCENARIO AND COMING UP WITH ALTERNATIVE WAYS OF REACTING IN ORDER TO BREAK AN ESCALATING CHAIN OF EVENTS

The worksheet is meant to be used landscape with the sheet title on the right. In this orientation the chain goes top left to bottom right. IGNORE THE SPIKY SHAPE.

The first objective is to come up with a conflict scenario that is typical of what might happen in school using fictional characters and made-up names. This can be used either as a teacher-led whole-class activity or with pupils working individually or in pairs.

If working on one whole-class scenario discuss:

- if there is just one instigator who is to blame;
- if the other party(ies) also carry some responsibility;
- who carries the greatest responsibility;
- if bystanders also carry some responsibility for not intervening; and
- if a genuine misunderstanding is the root cause.

If working in pairs or individually, quickly go through a few scenarios which are 'different' from proceeding ones.

Now draw attention to the spiky box; it is a 'chain breaker'. Ask the pupils to decide where and how the chain could have been broken by putting a cross on an arrow and joining the previous link to an alternative action written in the chain-breaker shape.

PLENARY

A chain breaker is an action or reaction which defuses a situation or simply breaks off the escalating chain of events. One party walking away or saying 'Forget it' could be a chain breaker.

In each scenario there will be more than one place where a chain breaker could be used.

Chain breaking prevents conflict, shows maturity and prevents unpleasant consequences.

UNIT 36: CHAIN BREAKERS

UNIT 37: BULLYING IS...

MAIN FOCUS: DEFINING WHAT CONSTITUTES BULLYING.

Discuss whether or not bullying is always/usually/sometimes/occasionally perpetrated by individuals or groups. Discuss if the groups act as one or as a number of individuals.

Raise the matter of frequency – does one isolated incident constitute bullying? How often do incidents have to occur before it becomes bullying?

Is physical bullying worse than mental, or vice versa?

Take a look at the worksheet. In the centre are a few examples of what might be regarded as bullying. At the top are boxes denoting perpetrators, individuals or groups and at the bottom is a row of boxes denoting frequency.

The task is to use coloured lines to link up an incident to boxes which would make that incident an act of bullying. For example, one might link 'Using an offensive nickname' to both top boxes and to 'regular' and 'constant'.

It may be appropriate to allow working in pairs.

PLENARY

Go through each of the examples and compare how people have linked them. Is there a consensus regarding perpetrator(s)?

Is there agreement on the threshold frequency that identifies an action as bullying?

Does the threshold frequency vary according to action?

UNIT 37: BULLYING IS . . .

hiding someone's property

stealing property

grabbing property and withholding it

deliberately damaging property

poking, prodding or tapping

hitting, punching, slapping or kicking

ignoring or shunning

making threats

insulting

using an offensive nickname

taunting

done by a group

done by an individual

constant (several times each day)

regular (every day)

frequent (every week)

occasional (once a month)

once

UNIT 38: BULLIES ARE...

MAIN FOCUS: GETTING INTO THE MIND AND MOTIVATION OF A BULLY

Recap on the fact that bullying can be physical, mental or both.

Introduce the sheet as a way of looking at the character of a typical bully, taking care not to name names.

Go through the descriptors, establishing what each one means. Point out that some of the descriptors may not apply.

The task is to discuss the descriptors and use one colour to shade those that apply to all bullies, a second colour for those that apply to some, and a third colour for those that probably apply.

If appropriate, people can work in pairs and have their own (quiet) discussion.

At the bottom of the sheet is an oval for pupils to add their own descriptor to sum up all bullies.

Take a straw poll of who has marked each descriptor with which colour. Where there is not a clear consensus, ask individuals to say why they marked the descriptor as they did.

Attempt to come up with a definition of a bully.

PLENARY

Bullying is caused by bullies, not victims.

Bullies are often compensating for their own inadequacies or problems.

Bullies find it difficult to have genuine friendships.

No-one likes a bully.

UNIT 38: BULLIES ARE...

Bullies...

have lots of friends

don't have power over their life

are good to have as a friend

don't have any **real** friends

want to gain power over other people

are or have been bullied themselves

have parents who let them get away with anything

are good leaders

put others down in order to feel important

are very confident

are really insecure

have very strict, overbearing parents

have low self-esteem

make others look small to make themselves look big

are good achievers

are poor achievers

deserve our sympathy

are violent

deserve our respect

deserve our contempt

are cowards

are tough and brave

have a personality problem

have very poor social skills

need help

KEY: ⬭ all bullies
⬭ some bullies
⬭ probably some or all bullies

UNIT 39: WHO ARE THE VICTIMS?

MAIN FOCUS: SEEING BEYOND THE FALSE IMAGES PROJECTED BY BULLIES AND THEIR TARGETS, AND LOOKING FOR SIMILARITIES

The scale lines on this sheet require the positioning of a **B** to represent a bully and a **T** to represent their target. Choose to focus, first, on the persona of a typical bully or their target and complete all the scale lines before commencing on the other persona. You may want to invite pupils to *think* of a bully or target WITHOUT IDENTIFYING THEM.

Take each scale line, one at a time, and discuss, briefly, what the labels mean with regard to the bully/target. Pause after each to allow the pupils to place their letter symbol on the scale.

Start again with the first scale line, discussing the other persona.

When everyone has completed, look at each scale in turn and ascertain which is the commonest placing for the bully and the target. Make a whole-group sheet based upon the consensus.

Examine the consensus sheet – what is the balance between the right-hand positive side, the left-hand negative side and the pretend zone in the middle? Are there areas where the bully and the target are similar?

PLENARY

People often try to project a false image of themselves to hide aspects they are not happy with or are ashamed of. Some of these people are more convincing than others. Bullying cannot be stopped if targets hide it and witnesses do nothing.

'The only thing necessary for the triumph of evil is for good men to do nothing.'
Edmund Burke, 1729–97, British political writer and statesman

'Throughout history, it has been the inaction of those who could have acted; the indifference of those who should have known better; the silence of the voice of justice when it mattered most; that has made it possible for evil to triumph.'
Haile Selassie

UNIT 39: WHO ARE THE VICTIMS?

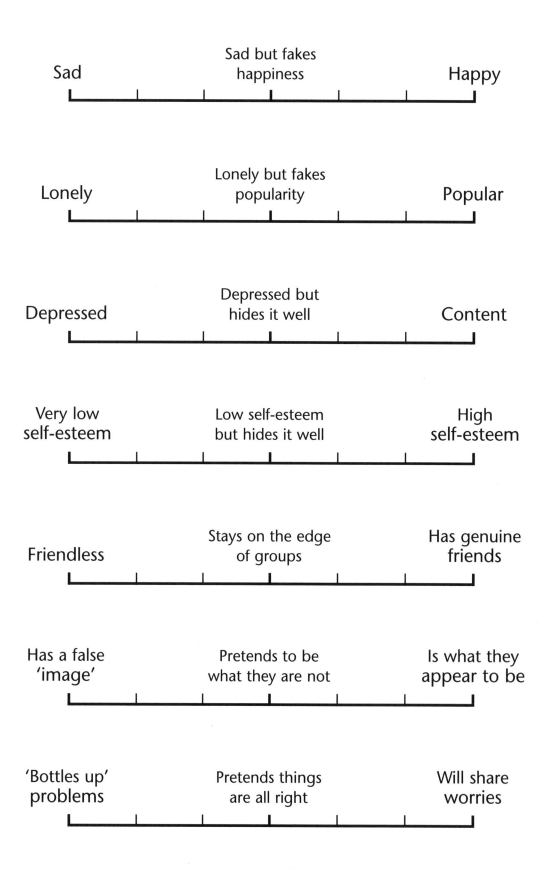

Sad	Sad but fakes happiness	Happy
Lonely	Lonely but fakes popularity	Popular
Depressed	Depressed but hides it well	Content
Very low self-esteem	Low self-esteem but hides it well	High self-esteem
Friendless	Stays on the edge of groups	Has genuine friends
Has a false 'image'	Pretends to be what they are not	Is what they appear to be
'Bottles up' problems	Pretends things are all right	Will share worries

UNIT 40: RESPONDING TO BULLIES

MAIN FOCUS: DIFFERENT WAYS, BOTH POSITIVE AND NEGATIVE, OF RESPONDING TO VERBAL AND PHYSICAL BULLYING

Begin with sheet 40(a) and clarify what is meant by verbal taunts – insults and remarks intended to hurt or provoke the targeted victim.

Discuss perceived levels of seriousness, insulting nicknames, so-called 'jokes', offensive names and jibes, insults aimed at family members, race, religion etc.

Discuss the cumulative effect of constant, sustained and orchestrated abuse on a person's life.

Discuss the range of possible responses on the sheet. Use a colour code to mark those which *might* make the situation worse or better, and those not likely to change anything.

Are there other suggestions from the group?

Take sheet 40(b) and define physical assaults as including: throwing things at someone, poking, hitting, kicking, pushing etc.

Again look through the suggestions and identify those which will or will not make a difference.

Which *might* make the situation worse? Why?

Is doing nothing really an option?

What could the consequences of doing nothing be for (a) the bully(ies) and (b) for present and future victims?

PLENARY

Doing nothing is not a solution; it encourages the situation to continue.

People in authority are powerless to stop it if they don't know what's going on.

We all have a responsibility to stamp out bullying, but do we have the courage?

UNIT 40(a): RESPONDING TO BULLIES

Verbal taunts

Pretend you didn't hear

Do nothing and 'bottle up'

Retaliate with insults

Ignore and dismiss it

Retaliate with violence

Mockingly agree

Leave or run away

Bounce the insult back

Ask them to stop

Ask friends to ask them to stop

Suffer in silence

Pretend it doesn't bother you

Encourage them to pick on someone else

Speak to a friend about it

Speak to a teacher about it

Report it to someone in authority

Phone Childline (0800 1111)

Speak to family about it

UNIT 40(b): RESPONDING TO BULLIES

Physical assaults

Pretend you didn't notice

Do nothing and 'bottle up'

Retaliate with insults

Accept it as 'normal'

Retaliate with violence

Ask someone to 'get them back' for you

Leave or run away

Plan revenge

Ask them to stop

Ask friends to ask them to stop

Offer bribes if they will stop

Find some new, bigger 'friends'

Encourage them to pick on someone else

Speak to a friend about it

Speak to a teacher about it

Report it to someone in authority

Phone Childline (0800 1111)

Speak to family about it

ANGER MANAGEMENT PROGRAMME

Anger Management Programme

Pupil:

Group:

Start Date:

Review Date:

Duration: **6 sessions**

Session and date	Session objective	Activities	Resources	Outcomes/modifications
1	Listen to what your body is telling you.	Identify physical reactions to watch out for. Relate them to 'fight or flight' caveman response. How to we respond to the signs?	*Getting to Know Me* Unit 24	
2	Identify triggers that cause anger. Identify the 'wind-ups' that trigger an angry response in you.	Brainstorm possibilities, both silly and sensible Identify the remote control buttons which do or don't affect you. Add new buttons. Discuss how to 'block' the signal and add other methods.	Large sheet of paper or whiteboard *Getting to Know Me* Unit 28 *Getting to Know Me* Unit 29	
3	Did they mean to offend you?	Discuss how quick we can be to decide why someone did something. We don't **know**, we assume we know Alternative ways of viewing a situation.	*Getting to Know Me* Unit 27	

ANGER MANAGEMENT PROGRAMME

Anger Management Programme

Start Date:
Review Date:
Duration: **6 sessions**

Pupil:

Group:

Session and date	Session objective	Activities	Resources	Outcomes/modifications
4	Using your anger in a positive way.	What to do. What not to do. Discuss other ideas.	*Getting to Know Me* Unit 30	
5	Responding to an incident.	Passive. Confrontational/aggressive. Consult an arbiter. Negotiate.	*Getting to Know Me* Unit 25 and 26	
6	Social interaction skills.	Assess own use of eye contact, continuity nods/responses, questioning, agreement/disagreement. Assess extent to which we like others to apply these techniques.	*Getting to Know Me* Unit 18(a) *Getting to Know Me* Unit 18(b)	

BLANK PROGRAMME SHEET

Pupil:

Group:

Programme

Start Date:
Review Date:
Duration:

Session and date	Session objective	Activities	Resources	Outcomes/modifications

BEHAVIOUR CONTRACT

The school acknowledges that:

- the school exists so that pupils can learn
- all pupils and staff have a right to a safe working environment
- all pupils and staff have a right to be treated with respect
- all pupils and staff are responsible for what they do

The school undertakes to:

- provide learning experiences to suit your needs
- provide a safe environment for all pupils
- encourage you and all other pupils to try your best
- recognise and celebrate good behaviour
- recognise and celebrate achievements

I acknowledge that:

- all pupils have a right to learn
- all pupils and staff have a right to a safe working environment
- all pupils and staff are worthy of respect
- how I behave is a matter of my choice
- I am responsible for the choices I make

I undertake to:

- respect the safety and rights of all pupils and staff
- allow all pupils and staff to do their work
- behave in a sensible and responsible manner
- try my best and to seek help if I am unsure of what to do
- complete the classwork and homework required of me

signed ....

date...

on behalf of...

....School

signed ....

date..

Witnessed by ....

(signed)

....

(printed name)